Printed in the United States of America

First Printing, 2025

Break Every Chain, LLC
Sygardner41@yahoo.com

Library of Congress has catalogued the paperback Edition as follows:

Adventures of Sable Brown ~ Ruth Mohan by Shalise Y. Gardner
Includes Citizenship – United States, Authorship: Text and Artwork.

TXu 2-537-160

ISBN: 979-8-234-01228-9

*This book belongs to*

______________________________

One day when Sable was watching her favorite cartoon. A commercial came on about little girls and boys not having a mommy and a daddy. Sable looked at the television with tears in her eyes.

Sable ran to her mother, who was in the yard planting flowers.

"Mommy," cried Sable,
"I just watched a commercial
that showed little girls and boys
not having a mommy and a daddy."

Mommy, who's name is Sadie Brown, stopped what she was doing and hugged Sable tight. "I know it is sad to see children on television not having a mommy and a daddy, and living with people they don't know," said Sadie.

“I wish all children had a mommy and a daddy or someone that will love them forever,” Sable said.

Sable runs to her bedroom; Sammie follows behind her.

Sable closes her bedroom door behind Sammie. “Come on Sammie, we have to see Dr. Smooh,” said Sable. Into the closet they went.

Pushing through her clothes, Sable and Sammie see Dr. Smooh and they all hug each other.

Dr. Smooh already knew how Sable was feeling. "I'm going to take you two on an adventure to meet a new friend," Dr. Smooh said.

Dr. Smooh waved his wand at Sammie, and he could talk more. Dr. Smooh waved his wand again and off they went.

The first and only stop was at Ruth Mohan's house. Dr. Smooh, Sable and Sammie met Ruth on her front lawn.

"Hello Ruth, my name is Dr. Smooh, this is Sable and her brother Sammie. We want to talk to you about being adopted," said Dr. Smooh.

"Hi Sable, hi Sammie, yes let me tell you, my story. My name is Ruth Mohan, and I was born in Trinidad and Tobago. My nationality is Trinidadian and West Indian. My birth mommy couldn't take care of me. So, I was adopted by a new family. My current mom and dad couldn't have children, so they decided to adopt," Ruth explained.

Dr. Smooh butted in, "There's a process that parents must go through before they can start the adoption process. There are hundreds of thousands of children who need a family to love, and the goal is to give each child a loving home."

Ruth, can you tell Sable and Sammie how you feel as an adoptee?" asked Dr. Smooh.

"My current mommy and daddy adopted me when I was a baby. When I was 5 years old, they explained to me that I was adopted. I felt sad, angry, confused, lost, scared, fearful, upset, worthless and alone. I didn't understand why my birth mommy and birth daddy couldn't take care of me," said Ruth.

“That’s so sad,” said Sammie.

Dr. Smooh said, "A lot of children come from different countries to be adopted, they see how different they are from their current family, and they don't understand."

An adoptee that is born in another country, comes to America as a baby, is stripped of his or her culture by the age of 12. Most of the children do not speak their native language. That is why Ruth does not have an accent when she speaks," explained Dr. Smooh.

"When I get older, I want to go back to Trinidad and Tobago to find my birth mommy and birth daddy. It is not about being happy to find my birth mommy and birth daddy. It's about being complete and getting some understanding," Ruth expressed.

"Yes, I think you should go Ruth," said Sable.

“When I meet new kids, they ask me was I adopted and what does that mean? I try to explain the positives and negatives of being adopted,” Ruth said sadly.

“Sometimes when I go out with my adopted mommy and daddy, and I see people who look like me. I wonder if they’re my mommy and daddy,” said Ruth.

"I am very happy with my current mommy and daddy. They show me love, they gave me a home to live in and they encourage me to be the best that I can be," expressed Ruth.

"Every adoptee has a voice that needs to be heard.
Every adoptee deserves a loving and understanding family.
Adopted parents should not deny the children of their culture and the want to search for their biological mommy and daddy," affirmed Dr. Smooh.

"Thank you so much for explaining your truth, Ruth," said Dr. Smooh.

"I've learned that it's Ok to not be Ok as an adoptee," said Ruth.

"Ruth, you are my new friend," Sable said.
"You are mine too!" shouted Sammie.

"Ok, Sable and Sammie, I must take you two back home,"
Dr. Smooh anxiously said.

Sable, Sammie and Dr. Smooh waved goodbye to Ruth and her mommy and daddy.

Dr. Smooh waved his wand and changed Sammie's speech back. Sable and Sammie waved goodbye to Dr. Smooh, back through the closet they went!

“This turned out to be a good day,” Sable said to Sammie.

“Yes,” Sammie said.

"I think I'll go watch another commercial," Sable laughed.
"Me too," shouted Sammie.

# Things to Never Say to an Adoptee ~

"Be glad you were chosen or picked."

"You're lucky to be adopted."

# Things to Never Say to an Adoptee ~

For more information regarding adoption, contact your local adoption agencies or community supportive services in your city.

# *Dedication*

*This book is dedicated to Adoptees,
we hear you!*

# Acknowledgement

*I would like to thank God for blessing me with a creative imagination*

*and to Ruth Mohan for sharing her story.*

www.ingramcontent.com/pod-product-compliance
Lightning Source LLC
LaVergne TN
LVHW070159110826
845147LV00002B/442

* 9 7 9 8 2 3 4 0 1 2 2 8 9 *